Years 3-4

This book is for pupils studying KS2 History
in Years 3 and 4 (ages 7-9).

It's full of facts, sources and questions covering
'Changes in Britain from the Stone Age to the Iron Age'
— perfect for exploring and understanding the whole topic.

Picture acknowledgements

Cover photo: Private Collection / © English Heritage Photo Library / Bridgeman Images.

p2 - p9

p3 (skull) © Mary Evans / Natural History Museum. p4 (Ötzi), © akg-images / Johann Brandstetter. p4 (dagger) South Tyrol Museum of Archaeology, Bolzano, Italy / Wolfgang Neeb / Bridgeman Images. p4 (cap) South Tyrol Museum of Archaeology, Bolzano, Italy / Wolfgang Neeb / Bridgeman Images. p5 (flint tool) © Mary Evans / Natural History Museum. p6 (map) Adapted from UK Happisburgh c. 800000 map by Philg88. This work is licensed for re-use under the Creative Commons Attribution 4.0 International licence http://creativecommons.org/licenses/by/4.0/deed.en. p6 (Happisburgh scene) © John Sibbick. p7 (male scientist) © RGB Ventures / SuperStock / Alamy. p8 (tools) © Mary Evans / Natural History Museum. p8 (Boxgrove) © English Heritage / Mary Evans. p9 (skull) De Agostini Picture Library / Bridgeman Images. p9 (teeth) National Museum of Wales.

p10 - p19

p10 (Paviland burial) National Museum of Wales. p11 (engraved bone) © The Trustees of the British Museum. p12 (Stone Age huts) © iStockphoto.com/ TT. p12 (barbed points) © Mary Evans / Natural History Museum. p13 (Mesolithic hut) Bildarchiv Steffens / Bildarchiv Steffens / Ralph Rainer Steffens / Bridgeman Images. p13 (antler head dress) © The Trustees of the British Museum. p14 (skeleton) © David Wall / Alamy. p14 (reconstruction) © Mary Evans / Natural History Museum. p14 (LHS cave painting) © Mary Evans/J. Bedmar/Iberfoto. p14 (RHS cave painting) © Mary Evans/P. Rotger/Iberfoto. p15 (fish trap) Mesolithic fish trap: National Roads Authority. Photography by John Sunderland. p16 (footprint) © M Bell, Reading University. p16 (coastal scene) © Crown copyright Historic Scotland reproduced courtesy of Historic Scotland. www.historicscotlandimages.gov.uk. p17 (tsunami deposits) Storegga tsunami deposits by Stozy10 licenced for re-use under the creative commons licence http://creativecommons.org/licenses/by/3.0/deed.en. p18 (sickle) © World History Archive / Alamy. p18 (wheat) © Steve Cavalier / Alamy. p18 (pottery bowl) © The Trustees of the British Museum. p18 (cloth) Copyright: Petrie Museum of Egyptian Archaeology, University College London - UC 72770. p19 (skull) Photo by Dr Rick Schulting used with permission from The Duckworth Laboratory , University of Cambridge. p19 (spine) From Rib lesions in skeletons from early neolithic sites in Central Germany: On the trail of tuberculosis at the onset of agriculture. Nicole Nicklisch et al. Copyright © 2012 Wiley Periodicals, Inc.

p20 - p29

p20 (group of houses) © Peter Phipp/Travelshots.com / Alamy. p20 (house interior) © Realimage / Alamy. p21 (chipped flint tools) De Agostini Picture Library / A. Dagli Orti / Bridgeman Images. p21 (polished flint tools) De Agostini Picture Library / A. Dagli Orti / Bridgeman Images. p22 (building Stonehenge) Reconstruction artwork of Stonehenge being built © English Heritage. p23 (building Stonehenge) © Look and Learn. p23 (Durrington Walls remains) photo by: Mike Pitts. p24 (Grimes Graves, Norfolk) © Skyscan Photolibrary / Alamy. p24 (Neolithic flint mine) © Heritage Image Partnership Ltd / Alamy. p25 (working copper) © Look and Learn. p25 (copper ore) © iStockphoto.com/chriscrowley. p25 (copper tools) De Agostini Picture Library / A. de Gregorio / Bridgeman Images. p25 (bronze tools) © The Art Archive / Alamy. p26 (Amesbury Archer) by Pasicles licenced for re-use under the Creative Commons CC0 1.0 Universal Public Domain Dedication http://creativecommons.org/publicdomain/zero/1.0/deed.en. p26 (gold ornaments) © Wessex Archaeology. p27 (the companion) © Wessex Archaeology. p27 (grave goods) © Wessex Archaeology. p28 (working metal) © Look and Learn. p29 (gold cape) © David Pimborough / Alamy. p29 (amber beads) © Wessex Archaeology.

p30 - p39

p30 (pots) © Cambridge Archaeological Unit . p30 (hut reconstructon) © Holmes Garden Photos / Alamy. p31 (cloth) © Cambridge Archaeological Unit. p32 (offerings) © Museum of London, UK / Bridgeman Images. p33 (hillfort) Reconstruction drawing of Woodhouse Hillfort, Cheshire by Dai Owen © Cheshire West and Chester Borough Council. p33 (man) © English Heritage Photo Library / Bridgeman Images. p34 (tools) Ashmolean Museum, University of Oxford, UK/Getty Images. p35 (Iron Age family) © English Heritage Photo Library / Bridgeman Images. p36 (hillfort — aerial view) © Robert Harding Picture Library Ltd / Alamy. p36 (hillfort) © English Heritage Photo Library / Bridgeman Images. p37 (skulls) © Hampshire County Council Arts & Museums Service. p37 (sword) © The Trustees of the British Museum. p38 (map) © iStockphoto.com/duncan1890.

Contents

Published by CGP

Written by Joanna Copley

Editors: Katie Braid, Camilla Simson

Reviewers: Janet Berkeley, Maxine Petrie

ISBN: 978 1 78294 195 8

With thanks to Katherine Faudemer and Hayley Thompson for the proofreading.

With thanks to Laura Jakubowski for the copyright research.

Printed by Elanders Ltd, Newcastle upon Tyne

Clipart from Corel®

History and Prehistory

History is the study of the past. When we learn about history we learn about what happened in the past and why those things happened. We discover what people and places were like and how they've changed over time.

What important events that have happened in the past can you think of?

Before history began

Nowadays, most people in Britain can write. But that wasn't always the case. People lived in Britain for hundreds of thousands of years before anyone started writing. There's a special term for the period of time before people started writing. It's called prehistory. Prehistory lasted for a really, really long time.

'Pre' means 'before', so prehistory means 'before history'.

We think that people have been in Britain for nearly 1 million years. The first writing that's been found is only about 2000 years old. So the length of time that people in Britain have been writing is tiny compared to the length of prehistory.

First people in Britain | PREHISTORY | First writing in Britain

| 1 million years ago | 750 000 | 500 000 | 250 000 | Today |

Discovering the past

Historians and archaeologists are people who study history and prehistory. They look for evidence (clues) to work out what happened and what life was like in the past.

What evidence do you think historians and archaeologists use to find out about the past?

There are lots of different kinds of evidence that are used to find out about the past. Sometimes people in the past wrote things down or drew pictures — these give us lots of information. Archaeologists have found drawings on cave walls and carved pictures from thousands of years ago. They've also found things like bones, tools, clothes and jewellery.

The sources of knowledge

The pieces of evidence used to work out what happened in the past are called sources. Sources can be primary sources or secondary sources.

Primary sources are <u>from</u> the period of time that's being studied.

This skull was found in Gough's Cave in Cheddar Gorge. It's about <u>9000 years old</u>, and it's a <u>primary</u> source. Archaeologists can find out things about the past by studying it. For example, there's a hole in the skull that could give them information about how this person <u>died</u>.

<u>Secondary sources</u> aren't from the time that's being studied, but they still give us <u>information</u> about the past. These history books are <u>secondary</u> sources — they've got lots of information about the past in them, but they're not <u>from</u> the past.

The search goes on

Archaeologists and historians are always looking for <u>new sources</u>. Finding new sources gives them <u>more information</u>, which lets them build up a better picture of what life used to be like. Sometimes it might even <u>change their minds</u> about something they <u>thought</u> they knew.

Why might new sources change people's ideas about what happened in the past?

So, what's in this book then?

This book looks at Britain from the <u>Stone Age</u> to the <u>Celts</u> and finds out what life was like for the people who lived in <u>prehistoric Britain</u>. It was quite different from your life today!

How We Discover Prehistory

Archaeologists find out about the past by digging.

Can you think why archaeologists might need to dig to find out about the past?

Evidence is out there...

We don't know a lot about prehistory — evidence of what life was like that long ago can be difficult to find. Usually only very hard things are left after thousands of years — things like stone tools and arrowheads. If archaeologists are lucky though, they can find human bones too, like the skull on the previous page.

Ötzi the Ice Man – frozen in time

Sometimes softer materials do survive, but they often have a sad story to tell...

"I'm Ötzi. I lived around the snowy mountains of Italy. I wore clothes made of fur and animal skin and had tools like daggers that I made myself."

Archaeologists think Ötzi was alive around 5300 years ago. When he was about 45 years old, he died in the mountains. Snow fell on him, and his body quickly froze. This meant that his body, clothes and equipment were kept safe for us to discover. Sad for Ötzi... but interesting for us.

Ötzi was found with this dagger and cap.

How old is the evidence?

Archaeologists need to work out how old the things they find are.

Here are three ways they can do this:

1. Studying carbon atoms.

Every living thing contains carbon atoms. A special form of these atoms begins to decay (break down) when the thing dies. Scientists can tell how old things like plant remains or bones are by looking at how much of this type of atom is left.

2. Seeing how deep they're buried.

Archaeologists dig down into the ground. The things at the top are newer, and the things deeper down are older.

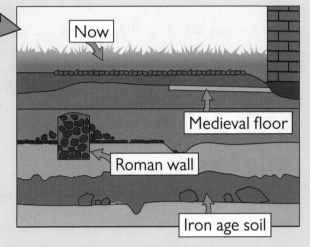

Now

Medieval floor

Roman wall

Iron age soil

3. Looking at what they're buried with.

If stone tools are in the same layer as bones or plants, they come from the same time, so scientists can work out how old they are.

Look at this stone tool. How do you think archaeologists worked out how old it is?

To find out how old tools like this are, archaeologists can look at how deep they're buried and look at what they're buried with. They can also compare them to other tools of the same type. Humans started with simple tools, which got more and more complicated.

*Can you guess how old this tool is?**

The 3 Ds of archaeology — dig, discover, date

Ötzi was a really amazing discovery. After all, it's not every day that you come across a 5300 year old mummy — imagine how exciting it must have been to find him! Now that you know how we find out about prehistory, it's time to look at what we've found out about prehistoric Britain. Turn the page to learn about the first people who lived here...

*It's around 680 000 years old!

The First People in Britain

Timeline

Happisburgh people .... THE STONE AGE .... Modern humans in Africa | Modern humans in Europe

1 million years ago | 750 000 | 500 000 | 250 000 | Today

The <u>black lines</u> on this map show what the coastlines of Britain and Europe look like <u>today</u>. The <u>green areas</u> show what the land looked like almost <u>one million years ago</u>.

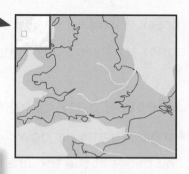

How was the land different one million years ago?

How do you think people would have travelled to Britain from Europe?

The first Britons?

At a place called Happisburgh we have found stone tools, animal bones and teeth, and plant remains possibly as much as <u>950 000 years old</u>. That's nearly a million years old! The stone tools are the <u>earliest evidence</u> of people in Britain that's been found.

The period of time these tools are from is called the Stone Age, because we think that the people alive then used mostly <u>stone tools</u> — they didn't use any metal. An artist has drawn what life might have been like for Happisburgh people in the Stone Age.

What animals can you see? What tools are the people using?
What are they eating? Have they cooked their food?
What evidence do you think the artist used to make this picture?

A different sort of human

We don't know exactly what the Happisburgh people were like, as we haven't found any of their bones yet. But we know that they weren't exactly the same as us. Humans that look like we do now first lived about 200 000 years ago in Africa. They didn't arrive in Europe till about 60 000 years ago.

All humans belong to a group called hominins. Hominins that look like we do now are called Homo sapiens.

And then they were gone...

We know that the people who lived at Happisburgh didn't stay in Britain.

Why do you think they might they have left Britain?

These scientists may have the answer.

"I'm Cathy and I look at long cores (tubes) drilled out of the sea bed. The remains of organisms in the layers of mud and sand show when the climate got warmer or colder."

"I'm Alex and I'm holding an ice core drilled out from deep inside an ice sheet. I find out about the past by studying layers in the ice. Every time snow falls it makes a different layer. These layers can tell us about the climate when the snow fell."

Scientists like Cathy and Alex have found evidence that the climate of the world changed. The weather got colder, the ice came down from the north, and we had glacial periods. In a glacial period, the land was covered in glaciers. This may have driven people further south, where it was warmer.

The Happisburgh people – the very first Britons?

People lived at Happisburgh nearly a million years ago. They may not have been the first people who lived in Britain but they're the first ones we've found evidence of. There's plenty of evidence of people after this time though. Turn the page to find out more...

Early Humans in Britain

Timeline

Happisburgh people	Early stone tools	Boxgrove Man	Swanscombe Woman	Pontnewydd People
1 million years ago	750 000	500 000		250 000	Today

The glaciers came and went over thousands of years. The times in between glacial periods, when the ice had melted and the weather was warmer, are called interglacial periods. Small numbers of people moved around Stone Age Britain in the interglacial periods. We know they were there because we've found clues like these <u>tools</u>. They're about 700 000 years old.

What do you think these stone tools might have been used for?

Now let's discover the <u>earliest human remains</u> found in Britain.

The bones of Boxgrove Man

<u>Boxgrove Man</u> is the remains of a human found in Boxgrove, in the south-east of England. He's not a modern human — he's a 'Homo heidelbergensis'. At the Boxgrove site, you can see where he might have sat and made tools, <u>500 000 years ago</u>.

What are the people doing in this picture? Can you see anyone using any stone tools?

The skull of Swanscombe Woman

These are some pieces of a human skull.

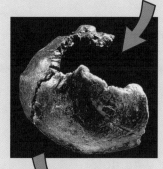

They were found in Swanscombe,
in Kent (south-east England).
They belonged to a <u>woman</u> who lived
about <u>400 000 thousand years ago</u>.

At this time there were lions, rhinos, monkeys and elephants roaming around Britain.

Swanscombe woman was a bit bigger and stronger than us. She'd have needed to be!

Male or female?

Archaeologists can sometimes tell whether bones belonged to a <u>man</u> or a <u>woman</u>.
Some bones, like the skull, are slightly different in men and women. The <u>pelvis</u> is
also quite different. The picture below shows a man's pelvis and a woman's pelvis.

Which pelvis do you think belongs to a man and which belongs to a woman?

Did you think the wider one would be the man's? Well, it's not!
In fact, women have a wider pelvis to make childbirth easier.

The people of Pontnewydd

The remains of at least five people were found at Pontnewydd in Wales.
They lived about <u>230 000 years ago</u>.

These teeth are from one of the Pontnewydd people.
One of the teeth is a <u>milk tooth</u>.

What does this tell us about the person the teeth belonged to?

Three sets of remains... but what happened in-between?

We haven't found any human remains from between the times of Boxgrove Man,
Swanscombe Woman and the Pontnewydd people. Maybe no one lived here at those
times. We <u>don't know for sure</u> though, it could just be we haven't found the evidence yet.

Life in the Glacial Periods

Timeline

Happisburgh people ... Boxgrove Man ... Swanscombe Woman ... Pontnewydd People ... Paviland Man ... End of last glacial period

1 million years ago ... 750 000 ... 500 000 ... 250 000 ... Today

Archaeologists haven't found many human remains from the 200 000 years after the Pontnewydd people.

Do you think this means that there weren't any humans in Britain during this gap? Why or why not?

Evidence of human life...

We know that humans were around in Britain because we've found things like tools from around 100 000 years ago. From this, we can tell that people were in Britain for at least some of the time. The next oldest human skeleton that's been found is from 33 000 years ago. Let's find out about him. Or is it her...?

Paviland... Man?

Paviland Man was originally called 'The Red Lady' of Paviland. When he was discovered, people thought he was a woman, as he was buried with jewellery. But when his bones were studied he turned out to be a young man. Some people think that Paviland Man might have been killed hunting a mammoth, because a mammoth skull was found nearby. This painting shows what his burial might have looked like.

What can you see happening in the picture?

In what ways are the people in the picture like us?

How are they different to us?

Where do you think they got food and the materials for their clothes from?

Strange behaviour in the Cheddar Caves

Bones from around 14 700 years ago have been found in the caves in Cheddar Gorge.
There are animal bones that have <u>cut marks</u> from <u>stone knives</u> on them.
There are also <u>human bones</u> with
marks from knives on them.

What do you think this could mean?

It might mean that humans <u>ate</u> other humans. And it looks like they did because as well as
cut marks, there are also <u>tooth marks</u>, where the meat was nibbled away.

Nowadays most people believe that eating other humans is
<u>wrong</u>, but the people in the Cheddar Caves may not have
thought this — it might have been quite a <u>normal</u> thing to do!

Humans that eat other humans are called <u>cannibals</u>.

Can you think of any reasons why these people may have eaten other humans?

Art in the ages of ice

The object below is about 12 500 years old, and it's the oldest piece of art that's
been found in Britain. A picture has been engraved on it. Look at it very closely...

What do you think this is a picture of?*
What might it be drawn on?

The end of the age of ice

For hundreds of thousands of years, glaciers came and went. About <u>11 500 years ago</u> (a few
thousand years after the people who were found at Cheddar died) the glaciers melted for
the <u>last time</u>. The last glacial period was over.

Evidence of humans in the glacial periods is hard to find

There isn't much evidence of humans in these glacial periods left, so Paviland Man and the
Cheddar Cannibals are <u>important discoveries</u> — they give us clues to how people lived.
The glacial periods didn't last forever though — a new way of life was about to start...

*It's a picture of a horse. It's been engraved into a bone.

The Mesolithic

Timeline

| Happisburgh people | End of last glacial period | Star Carr | THE MESOLITHIC | End of the Mesolithic | | | | |

| 1 million years ago | 12 000 | 10 000 | 8000 | 6000 | 4000 | 2000 | Today |

The period of time after the last glacial period is called the 'Mesolithic'. Before the last glacial period, Britain was a place of <u>open grassland</u>. The picture below shows what Britain might have looked like in the <u>Mesolithic</u>.

How had the land changed?

How might the changes to the land have affected the types of plants and animals that lived in Britain?

The glaciers had left <u>lakes</u> and with warmer weather Britain became a land of <u>forest</u>. The forest was full of deer, boar, elk, and huge wild cattle. In the lakes there were fish and beaver to hunt. All you needed were the right <u>skills</u> and the right <u>tools</u> to catch them.

Hunters of the Mesolithic

People still used <u>stone tools</u> to hunt but they also used tools like these.

What do you think these tools are made of?
How do you think they might have been used for hunting?

These tools are made from <u>deer antlers</u>. They could have been used as <u>spears</u> to kill deer and boar, or as <u>harpoons</u> to kill fish in the lake.

A place to shelter

At Star Carr, in Yorkshire, archaeologists have found a settlement that was built by a lake. They think that people lived there some of the time, in <u>huts</u> that could have looked like this.

What do you think this hut is made of?

Why do you think the huts were built by a lake?

People still lived in <u>caves</u> too, or shelters that they <u>travelled with</u>. They still moved around, following the animals, and gathering different foods in different seasons.

Mesolithic humans – more like modern humans?

Were Mesolithic people like us? In many ways they were very like us. We know from fossils that they looked like us and we know that they lived in <u>families</u> and that they <u>cared for their families</u>. They may also have had <u>spiritual beliefs</u>, just like many people today.

Look at the picture on the left.

What do you think the picture shows?

It's an <u>antler head dress</u>. Historians think these were made and worn by the people who lived in Star Carr. They may have been used during rituals. If Mesolithic people had rituals, historians think it's likely that they had <u>spiritual beliefs</u>.

Can you think of any other reasons the people in Star Carr may have made head dresses like this?

Mesolithic Britain, another step towards modern man

So, Mesolithic people used tools to <u>hunt animals</u>, they <u>travelled</u> from place to place but sometimes lived in huts in <u>settlements</u>, and they probably had <u>spiritual beliefs</u>. Read on to find out what else was happening in Britain during the Mesolithic age...

Life in the Mesolithic

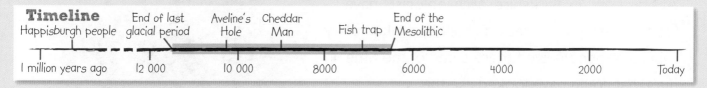

Timeline

Happisburgh people	End of last glacial period	Aveline's Hole	Cheddar Man	Fish trap	End of the Mesolithic				

1 million years ago	12 000	10 000	8000	6000	4000	2000	Today

It's likely that there were <u>only a few thousand</u> people in Britain during the Mesolithic, and that they were spread quite <u>far apart</u>.

How is this different to how Britain is today?

The Man in the Cave

The skeleton of <u>Cheddar Man</u> was found in Gough's Cave in Cheddar Gorge.

Cheddar Man is the oldest <u>complete</u> human skeleton to be found in Britain.

Archaeologists have recreated his face using his skeleton. They think that he looked like this.

Do you think Cheddar Man looks like people look today?

Furry friends and fierce creatures

We can tell what animals were around in the Mesolithic from <u>cave paintings</u>. These cave painting are from Spain.

What animals do you think were alive in the Mesolithic?

Why do you think these cave paintings were drawn?

We know from cave paintings in other places in Europe that as the climate warmed, mammoths had died out and other types of animals had become more common.

So what animals did Mesolithic people hunt? They would have hunted elk, boar, reindeer and wild cattle. They ate smaller animals like hedgehog, hare, and beaver too.

A balanced diet?

Meat wasn't the only food that Mesolithic people would have eaten.

What else do you think they might have eaten?

Mesolithic people were hunter-gatherers, so as well as hunting wild animals they would forage for wild plants. Scientists have found the pollen of some 'vegetable' plants in ancient soil, so we think Mesolithic people ate these. Some Mesolithic people probably ate fish too.

Archaeologists have found fish traps like this, which is evidence that people ate fish. They've also found piles of shells and fish bones around the coasts of Scotland and Ireland.

Graves in the gorge

The first human cemetery in Britain (that we know of) was dug up at Aveline's Hole, near Cheddar Gorge. It's about 10 300 years old. Mesolithic people were sometimes buried with some of their possessions, such as ornaments, and also tools and food.

Some people were buried with things like necklaces made of animal teeth!

Historians think this shows that these people believed in an afterlife. Why?

Cheddar Gorge is a hotspot for clues to Mesolithic life

Cheddar Gorge has given us the oldest whole human skeleton in Britain and the oldest cemetery in Britain. These, along with cave paintings, fish traps and other evidence have helped historians to build up a picture of what life was like for Mesolithic people.

Changes in the Mesolithic

Timeline

| Happisburgh people | End of last glacial period | Cheddar Man | Flooding of Doggerland | Goldcliff footprints | End of the Mesolithic | | | | |

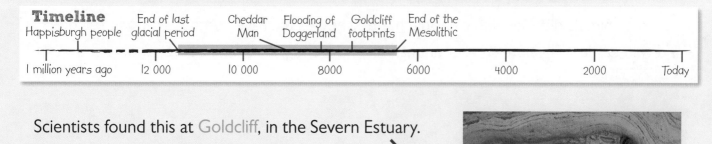

| I million years ago | 12 000 | 10 000 | 8000 | 6000 | 4000 | 2000 | Today |

Scientists found this at Goldcliff, in the Severn Estuary.

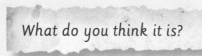

What do you think it is?

The Mesolithic life

Scientists think the picture above is a <u>footprint</u> from someone who lived at Goldcliff. Footprints like this one have been found from about 7500 years ago.

The picture below shows what life might have been like around this time.

What do you think these people ate?

How do you think they gathered their food?

How do you think they travelled from place to place?

Water, water, everywhere...

When the last glacial period ended, Britain was still joined to the rest of Europe by a low lying area called Doggerland.

As the <u>ice melted</u>, the <u>sea level had risen</u> causing low areas such as Doggerland to gradually <u>flood</u>. Then, around <u>8200 years ago</u>, a huge undersea shelf of <u>rock</u> off the coast of Norway suddenly <u>collapsed</u>. Tons and tons of rock fell to the sea floor, setting up a <u>great wave</u>.

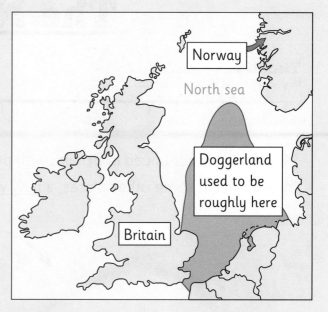

Do you know what a great wave like this is called?

A great wave like this is called a tsunami. This tsunami travelled down the North Sea. Some scientists think it caused the <u>final flooding of Doggerland</u>, leaving Britain as an <u>island</u>.

Show me the evidence...

Scientists think that the picture below shows <u>evidence</u> of the <u>tsunami</u>.

The picture shows layers of <u>peat</u> with a <u>layer of sand</u> in between. Scientists found this in Scotland. The <u>layer of sand</u> reached up to 50 miles inland and up to 4 metres above the usual tide line.

Why is this evidence of a tsunami?

Rising sea levels, a giant wave – an island nation is born

After the tsunami, Mesolithic life went on on the new island of Britain. People hunted, gathered plants, sewed clothes made from skins, and lived in huts or caves. But from now on, the only way for <u>new ideas</u> to come to Britain would be from <u>across the sea</u>.

The Neolithic

Timeline
Happisburgh people | End of last glacial period | T H E M E S O L I T H I C | Sickle from Iraq | Start of the Neolithic | End of the Neolithic

1 million years ago | 12 000 | 10 000 | 8000 | 6000 | 4000 | 2000 | Today

Mesolithic life continued in Britain, with people <u>hunting</u> animals and <u>gathering</u> other food. Meanwhile, in some other places, a <u>new way of life</u> had developed.

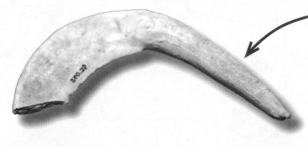

This picture shows a sickle — a hand-held tool used to <u>harvest</u> crops. It was found in Iraq and is around 7000 years old.

What does this tell us about how people in Iraq were getting food at this time?

A place to call home

Between 13 000 and 10 000 years ago, people in places outside of Britain began to <u>grow food deliberately</u>, instead of just gathering it where it was. They also domesticated animals, and used them as helpers or as food.

They also began to live in <u>towns</u>. For the first time, people didn't just have settlements that they rested in for a short time. Instead, they built places where they <u>stayed</u>. This meant they could sow and harvest their crops, and keep their animals nearby. This period of time has been called the Neolithic.

New skills, new things

Another difference between the Mesolithic and the Neolithic was the things that people <u>made</u>. Look at these two pictures.

What do you think the pictures show?

The Neolithic people made <u>pottery</u> and <u>woven material</u>. They still only had <u>stone tools</u> though (tools made of metal came later).

Death and destruction

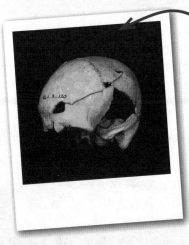

This picture shows a skull from the Neolithic. The person the skull belonged to may have died as a result of <u>fighting</u>.

Look at the skull. What's the evidence that they died because of fighting?

What do you think people might have been fighting over?

If the population of a settlement grows, <u>more space</u> is needed to grow food. If there's <u>not enough space</u>, then either the settlement has to move or the <u>land must be taken</u> from someone else. This could lead to <u>fighting</u>.

Deadly diseases

Fighting between tribes wasn't the only threat to Neolithic people. When people started living with animals, they started getting <u>diseases</u> that animals had. Some of these diseases were <u>deadly</u>. This picture shows the spine of someone who lived about 6000 years ago. It's collapsed. From this we can tell they had a disease called <u>tuberculosis</u>. Humans can get this disease from drinking infected cow's milk.

The changing times

So when did Britain start changing to a Neolithic way of life? Well, the first signs of change are from about <u>6500 years ago</u>. Historians haven't been able to agree on <u>why</u> people in Britain started living a Neolithic lifestyle though. It could be that the idea of farming <u>spread</u> to Britain, and people who were <u>already living here</u> started farming. Or it could be that people came from abroad, from places that <u>already</u> had a Neolithic lifestyle, and started farming in Britain.

Neolithic life changed Britain, but for better or worse?

A lot changed when Neolithic life came to Britain — people started living in <u>one place</u> rather than travelling around and they started <u>growing crops</u> and <u>keeping animals</u>. But this new way of life also brought problems — fighting broke out and diseases spread.

Neolithic Village Life

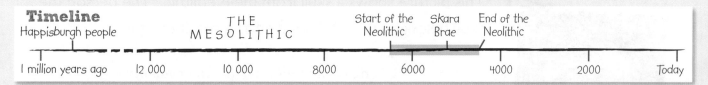

Timeline
Happisburgh people | THE MESOLITHIC | Start of the Neolithic | Skara Brae | End of the Neolithic

1 million years ago | 12 000 | 10 000 | 8000 | 6000 | 4000 | 2000 | Today

By <u>6000 years ago</u>, Britain had moved from Mesolithic to Neolithic. This meant big changes in how people lived.

Look at this picture. What do you think it shows?

A family home

The photo above is of Skara Brae in Orkney, Scotland. The remains of eight houses from about <u>5200 years ago</u> were found here. The houses were built by stacking flat rock together. They were roofed with wood and turf. There were no windows, just a smoke hole in the roof. Here's the inside of one house.

Can you guess what the different things in the house were used for?

There's a <u>stone dresser</u> on the right hand side of the house, which was used to keep belongings in. In the centre is the <u>hearth</u> — fires were lit here. The shallow stone boxes were <u>beds</u>, and the little stone tank by the dresser was used for <u>keeping fish bait</u>.

All for one and one for all

The houses in Skara Brae were all similar <u>sizes</u> and they were <u>connected</u> to a <u>sewer system</u>.

What do you think this might tell us about the importance of the people who lived there?

What does it tell us about the way they lived?

No one house is bigger, so it seems that the people who lived there were all <u>equal</u>. The fact that the houses were all connected to a sewer <u>system</u> suggests that the people worked <u>together</u> as a community. They may also have been concerned with hygiene!

What did the people in Skara Brae eat? We think they hunted deer, but they also kept sheep and cattle for meat. They trapped fish, collected cockles, mussels, oysters and clams. They also ate seabird eggs.

Tools of the trade

An important change in the Neolithic was the <u>stone tools</u> used. Until now, people had used <u>chipped</u> axes and tools like these.

Now people <u>ground</u> and <u>polished</u> their axes after chipping out the shape. This took many hours, but it meant that the tools were <u>stronger</u> and <u>handled better</u>.

Neolithic life – the good life?

From about <u>5000</u> to <u>4000 years ago</u>, many people in Britain lived like the people at Skara Brae. They built small <u>houses</u>, lived in small <u>family groups</u>, and ate a mixture of <u>farmed</u> and <u>hunted and gathered</u> food. Some historians think they also spent time making <u>art</u>.

Neolithic Stone Circles

Timeline

					Start of the Neolithic	Building of Stonehenge started		
Happisburgh people		THE MESOLITHIC						

1 million years ago	12 000	10 000	8000	6000	4000	2000	Today

People living in Britain in Neolithic times built stone circles like this one at Stonehenge. They were beginning to look to the <u>sky</u> — the <u>Sun</u>, the <u>Moon</u> and the <u>stars</u>.

What do you think stone circles like these were for?

Building the circles of stone

We think stone circles were used to mark <u>important days</u> in the year — the winter solstice and the summer solstice. These were the <u>shortest</u> and <u>longest days</u> of the year. Some stone circles were built so that the way the Sun shone on them showed <u>when</u> it was the <u>winter solstice</u> and when it was the <u>summer solstice</u>.

Why do you think these were important days to Neolithic people?

The winter solstice let them know <u>spring</u> was on its way. After the summer solstice, the <u>growing season</u> was over and the <u>harvesting season</u> began, followed by the winter. So the solstices were important dates for <u>farming</u> — they helped Neolithic people keep track of when to grow and harvest their crops.

How do you think they managed to build these great stone circles?

We aren't sure how the stone circles were built, but this picture and the one on the last page show some possible methods.

Stonehenge was built in stages over many hundreds of years. About 5000 years ago, a simple round ditch was built. Near the ditch were 56 pits. People were cremated here for hundreds of years.

About 4500 years ago, the big stone circle was started. This would have taken hundreds of people many years to put up.

It's party time!

People celebrated the winter solstice together with hog roasts. At Durrington Walls village site near Stonehenge, archaeologists have discovered the remains of burnt cattle and pigs. Many of the pig teeth found were from 9 month old animals — this suggests the animals were born in spring and killed at midwinter for a feast.

Read what life might have been like for someone who lived near Stonehenge...

"At Stonehenge we bury our dead, watch the sky, and communicate with ancestors in the afterlife. We live in Durrington, and visitors come to feast with us at the midwinter solstice. This is an important place for many people."

The stone circles of the Neolithic are a bit of a mystery...

We don't know for sure how or why the stone circles were built. We think they were to keep track of the seasons. That would make sense — now people were farming they needed to know when the seasons were changing so that they could grow their crops.

Flint, Copper and Bronze

Timeline

| Happisburgh people | THE MESOLITHIC | Start of the Neolithic | End of Stone Age, start of Copper Age | Start of Bronze Age |

| 1 million years ago | 12 000 | 10 000 | 8000 | 6000 | 4000 | 2000 | Today |

Flint is a hard, shiny rock. This picture shows an area of land in Norfolk where flint was found.

Can you guess why there are craters there?

Mining mayhem

In the Neolithic, people were using <u>flint tools</u>. The flint for these tools came from huge <u>flint mines</u> like the one in the picture below. Over 400 mining pits like this one were dug in the area of Norfolk shown above. That's why there are craters there now.

Look at this picture of a mining pit.

What do you think it was like in the pit?

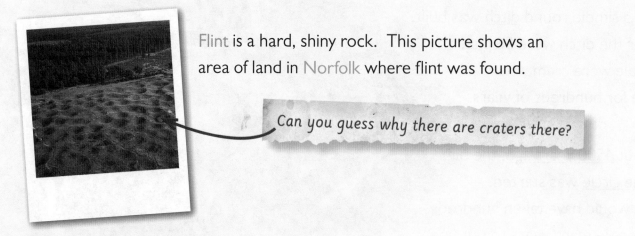

The mines were <u>dangerous places</u> — people died in them. It's likely that <u>children</u> were sent down into the dark to work in the smallest tunnels. Imagine having to do that!

How do you think you would have felt if you had worked down the mines?

Would you prefer to work down the mines or go to school? Why?

A talent worth having...

Look at this picture. What do you think the people are doing?

In Europe, people had a new way of making tools and weapons. They separated copper (a type of metal) from copper ore (a type of rock). It was then melted and poured into moulds, to cool and harden into tools and weapons. The people in the picture are making tools from copper.

copper ore

copper tools

In Britain, people started using copper about 4500 years ago as these new skills spread across the sea from Europe. This period of time is known as the Copper Age. Being able to work copper was a useful skill to have.

Apart from making your own tools, why do you think this skill was so useful?

Bronze is better

Copper is quite a soft metal. People learned that if it was mixed with tin, it became harder and stronger. A mixture of copper and tin is called bronze. People started making tools and weapons from bronze. The period of time when this happened is called the Bronze Age. In Britain, the Bronze Age started about 4000 years ago.

Say goodbye to stone tools...

So, people began to make tools and weapons from metals instead of just stone. This marked the end of the Stone Age. The Stone Age had gone on for millions of years so it was a big change. It changed the way people lived — as you'll see on the next few pages.

Life After the Stone Age

Timeline							

Timeline
Happisburgh people   THE MESOLITHIC   Start of the Neolithic   End of Stone Age   Amesbury Archer and Boscombe Bowmen

1 million years ago   12 000   10 000   8000   6000   4000   2000   Today

Archaeologists have found the <u>remains</u> of several people at Stonehenge. Some of these people were from near Stonehenge, but some were from <u>further away</u> — sometimes even <u>different countries</u>.

> Why do you think the remains of people from different countries were at Stonehenge?

Uncovering the Amesbury Archer

This skeleton is the Amesbury Archer, who lived about <u>4300 years ago</u>. Studies done on his teeth show that he came from near the Alps. He was buried near Stonehenge with many objects, including <u>flint arrowheads</u>, <u>copper knives</u> and the <u>gold hair ornaments</u> shown below.

> Historians think that the Amesbury Archer was a rich man. Why might they think that?

> How do you think the Amesbury Archer travelled from the Alps to Stonehenge?

Who is the Companion?

Near the grave of the Archer was the grave of a <u>younger man</u>.

He was found with hair ornaments like the Archer's and has been called the <u>Archer's companion</u>. Archaeologists believe he was raised in the south of England, but travelled further north as a teenager. They think he was in his twenties when he died.

Skeletal similarities

The Archer and the companion both had <u>unusual bones</u> in their feet.

What might this tell us about how the two men were connected?

Archaeologists think that the two men were <u>related</u>, because things like <u>unusual bones</u> are sometimes passed on in a family.

More visitors...

Another <u>grave</u> found near Stonehenge, at Boscombe Down, has the remains of several men, one teenager and some children in it. They weren't <u>from</u> Stonehenge — tests on their teeth show that they probably came from Wales.

These people have been named the 'Boscombe Bowmen'. This picture shows some of the things found in their grave. It shows one of several <u>pots</u>, plus other objects made of <u>flint</u> or <u>bone</u>.

Look carefully at the picture. Why do you think these people have been called the Boscombe Bowmen?

You can learn a lot from digging...

The Boscombe Bowmen, the Amesbury Archer and his companion give us lots of <u>clues</u> about life just after the Stone Age. They suggest people thought <u>Stonehenge</u> was an <u>important place</u>, they'd <u>travel long distances</u> to visit it, and often they'd travel in <u>families</u>.

Bronze Age Travel and Trade

Timeline
Happisburgh people

THE
MESOLITHIC

THE
NEOLITHIC

End of Stone Age
Start of Bronze Age

| 1 million years ago | 12 000 | 10 000 | 8000 | 6000 | 4000 | 2000 | Today |

People in the Bronze Age didn't have money to buy things — they <u>made</u> the things they needed. But there were some things that only <u>some</u> people could make.

How do you think Bronze Age people got the things they needed that they couldn't make themselves?

The rich and the poor

In the Bronze Age, for the first time in Britain, there was a difference between people who had many belongings, and people who didn't — the <u>rich</u> and the <u>poor</u>.

Look at the picture below.

Do you think the people in the picture would have been rich or poor? Why?

In the Bronze Age, the rich were the people who had <u>metal</u> and could make <u>objects</u> from <u>metal</u>. They could then swap these for other things they wanted. This is called <u>trading</u>.

Before, when there were only stone tools, everyone was <u>equal</u>. Now, if a person had <u>special skills</u> (like being able to work metal) and many things to trade, then they could be more <u>important</u> than others.

The people in the picture are working metal so they were probably <u>rich</u>.

An exciting find...

This cape is from around 3700 years ago.
It's made of gold and lined with leather.

What sort of person do you think would have owned a cape like this?

Travel and trade

A grave of a boy found near Stonehenge provides some evidence that people travelled and traded goods across Europe in the Bronze Age.

Archaeologists think this boy may have been from the Mediterranean. He was buried with a necklace made from these tiny amber beads. Archaeologists think that they came all the way from Scandinavia.

Trips to Britain...

We know that people were coming into Britain from abroad during the Bronze Age because of the graves that have been found — archaeologists can work out where these people were from by studying their teeth.

Other than their belongings, what else do you think these people brought to Britain?

People from abroad brought new skills and ideas with them — for example, they brought different ways of working with metal to Britain.

Get your metal detector and spade out...

...you never know what you might find! From the metalwork that's been discovered, historians can tell that trading was a big part of life for some people in Bronze Age Britain. We can also see that people travelled around and that there was a divide between people — some people were richer and more important than others.

Life in the Bronze Age

Timeline

Happisburgh people

THE MESOLITHIC

THE NEOLITHIC

Start of Bronze Age

First evidence of woven cloth

First evidence of wheels

1 million years ago   12 000   10 000   8000   6000   4000   2000   Today

Think about all of the things that you do on a normal day. For example, you might get up, have a shower, eat your breakfast, go to school in the car...

How do you think daily life was different for people in the Bronze Age?

Dirty dishes

Some of the best <u>evidence</u> for life in the Bronze Age comes from Flag Fen and Must Farm in the Fens. Objects like these pots have been found there, buried in mud.

Archaeologists have studied what's in the pots to see what people <u>ate</u>. It looks like Bronze Age people in the Fens ate <u>grain</u>, <u>fish</u> and <u>eels</u>.

For sale – one bedroom hut, lots of land...

This picture shows a reconstruction of a Bronze Age hut at Flag Fen.

What do you think the huts were made from?
What things did Bronze Age people need in order to survive?
Where do you think they got these things from?

Do you think this picture shows a good place to build a hut? Why or why not?

Families in the Bronze Age lived together in <u>huts</u>. The huts were built of wood plastered with mud and thatched with reeds or turfed (covered in grass). Bronze Age people <u>owned animals</u> and <u>made</u> or <u>grew</u> the things they needed, or <u>swapped</u> things with neighbours.

Getting around in the Bronze Age

How do you think people travelled around in the Bronze Age?

We know that Bronze Age people travelled on <u>foot</u> and by <u>boat</u>. They may have made boats by chopping down trees, hollowing them out and trimming them until they floated evenly. Inland, they could travel by river and on the coast they could paddle from bay to bay.

Archaeologists have also found part of a <u>wheel</u> from about 3000 years ago. It's the <u>oldest</u> wheel that's been found in England. Archaeologists think that it's <u>evidence</u> that people travelled in <u>other</u> ways during the Bronze Age — not just by boat or on foot.

What do you think the wheel tells us about transport in the Bronze Age?

New in this season...

What did people wear in the Bronze Age?
Well, by about 3900 years ago, <u>cloth</u> like this was being <u>woven</u> in Britain on looms. It was then made into <u>clothes</u>. Cloth <u>rots</u> away, so most cloth from this time <u>hasn't</u> survived.

Do you think that cloth like this could have been around before 3900 years ago?

Cloth like this could have been woven earlier than 3900 years ago.
We don't know because either it <u>hasn't survived</u> or we <u>haven't found it</u> yet.

A peaceful time – for now...

Bronze Age people lived in <u>huts</u> with their families and survived by <u>making</u> or <u>growing</u> the things they needed. Life at this time was peaceful, but things were about to change...

The End of the Bronze Age

From the middle of the Bronze Age to the end of the Bronze Age, the <u>weather</u> in Britain became a lot <u>colder</u> and <u>wetter</u>.

How do you think this bad weather affected people in Bronze Age Britain?

A bad forecast...

Changes in the weather can change what land can be used for. For example, historians think that Dartmoor was fertile land in the <u>early part</u> of the Bronze Age, but towards the end of the Bronze Age it became too <u>cold</u> and <u>wet</u> to farm there anymore.

Someone to blame...

About this time, at places all over Britain, people started <u>throwing bronze axes</u> and <u>swords</u> into local <u>streams</u> and <u>rivers</u>.

Why do you think people threw these things into the water?

Some archaeologists think that this was done as an <u>offering</u> to the <u>water spirits and gods</u> — they threw their valuable things into the water in exchange for <u>good weather</u>.

Tribal life

At the start of the Bronze Age most people lived with their families in <u>small groups</u>. Towards the end of the Bronze Age people started to make alliances with others and living in <u>tribes</u>, <u>not just families</u>.

Look at this picture. What do you think it shows?

Good views at the top

The picture above shows a hillfort. Some people built walls around the <u>tops of hills</u> to make forts and then farmed inside them. Sometimes the walls were made of earth, sometimes they were made of timber (wood) and stone.

Why do you think people started farming in hillforts?

The top of the hill was a good place to be. It was safer inside the walls, and people could see if anyone was coming to raid their camp, or take their animals.

Do you think you would have liked to belong to a tribe instead of just a family at this time? Why?

Safety in numbers...

At the start of the <u>Neolithic</u> (see pages 18-19), people <u>fought</u> over who could have <u>land</u> for farming. By the end of the Bronze Age, people had started fighting over who had the <u>best land</u>. If you belonged to a <u>big</u>, <u>strong</u> tribe, you could <u>protect</u> everything you owned.

The Celtic Age of Iron

Around 2700 years ago, a new age started in Britain — the Iron Age.

Why do you think this period of time was called the Iron Age?

Not just an age of iron

Some of the <u>oldest objects</u> made of <u>iron</u> that have been found in Britain were buried in Llyn Fawr, in Wales. Archaeologists found an <u>iron</u> sickle and an <u>iron sword</u> there that are about 2700 years old. The sickle and sword were found with some items made of <u>bronze</u>, including a giant bronze cauldron. This shows that around this time people used objects made of bronze as <u>well</u> as things made from iron.

Look at the Iron Age tools in this picture.

What do you think each tool is?
*What do you think each tool is made from?**

Better than bronze?

No-one is quite sure <u>why</u> people started making tools and weapons out of iron, rather than bronze. It could be that there was a <u>shortage of bronze</u>, so people started using iron instead and then found ways of making <u>better</u>, <u>cheaper</u>, <u>stronger</u> items from iron.

We still use steel to make lots of things today...

Iron on its own <u>isn't</u> any stronger than bronze. But if iron is <u>mixed</u> with a material called carbon, it makes a new material called <u>steel</u>. Steel is much stronger than bronze, so people could make better tools and weapons from it.

*The greenish tool is a <u>bronze</u> axe head. The next tool along is an <u>iron</u> axe head. Then there's a knife with a <u>bone</u> handle, a <u>bone</u> needle and awl, and a pair of <u>iron</u> shears.

The Celtic tribes

Iron Age people are often called Celts. The Celts were made up of a number of different tribes — they weren't just one group of people. This map shows the areas where some of the Celtic tribes lived.

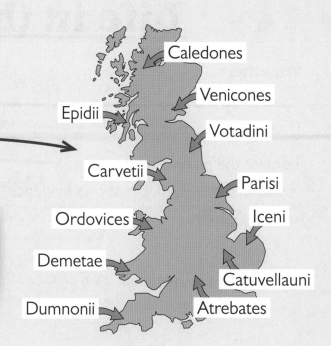

Caledones

Venicones

Epidii

Votadini

Carvetii

Parisi

Ordovices

Iceni

Demetae

Catuvellauni

Dumnonii

Atrebates

> There were also Celtic tribes in mainland Europe. The Gauls were Celts who lived in an area that included what we now call France.

A Celtic home

Look at this picture showing family life in the Iron Age.

> What can you see people doing in the picture?
> What things did this Celtic family own?

Here today, gone tomorrow...

We've found evidence of iron in Britain from about 2700 years ago. Iron gradually rusts away when it comes into contact with air and water, so there could have been iron in Britain earlier than this — either we haven't found it yet, or it's rusted away.

Life in the Iron Age

Look at the picture on the right.
It was taken in 2010, but shows evidence
of <u>Iron Age life</u>.

What do you think it's a picture of?

Evidence in the hills

The picture above shows the site of an Iron Age hillfort. It's the remains of Danebury Hillfort, in Hampshire. The picture was taken from the air, so you're looking down on the fort from above. Danebury Hillfort has given archaeologists lots of information about life in the Iron Age — they've spent <u>decades</u> studying it.

This picture shows what life might have been like inside Danebury Hillfort in the Iron Age.

What do you think life was like inside the fort?

How do you think people spent their time?

Disturbing the peace

These skulls were found at Danebury. They are all <u>damaged</u>. Archaeologists also found <u>burial pits</u>, where <u>many bodies</u> had been thrown in at once.

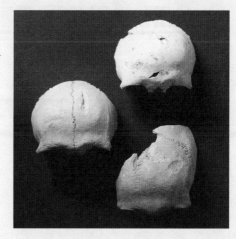

What do you think this evidence shows?

Archaeologists think that the skulls were damaged during fighting. The injuries could have been caused by spears, or other weapons.

Burial pits are sometimes used when lots of people die at the same time, like after fighting or during war. There's often no time or space to bury them separately.

So the damaged skulls and the burial pits could be <u>evidence</u> that there was <u>fighting</u> at the hillfort. Archaeologists think that life in the Iron Age was quite unsettled, and that fighting was common.

Artists and craftsmen?

Let's see what Iron Age people were like when they weren't fighting...

Look at this <u>sword handle</u> found from the Iron Age. The handle is made of 37 different pieces of bronze, iron, horn and glass.

What can you tell about the skills Iron Age people had by looking at this sword handle?

How do you think they would have made a sword like this?

Danebury Hillfort – a treasure trove of evidence

Lots of Iron Age hillforts have been found in Britain, but Danebury has given us some of the <u>best evidence</u> of life in the Iron Age. It was sometimes peaceful, sometimes violent, travel and trade continued, and people carried on learning new skills and making new things. But something was about to happen that would change life in Britain forever...

An Invasion from Rome

About 2000 years ago, the Iron Age was nearing its end. The people in Britain didn't know it yet, but life in Britain was about to change forever — the Romans were coming.

Have you heard of the Romans? What do you know about them?

A new power rises

The city of Rome, in what's now called Italy, was founded about <u>2750 years ago</u>. By about <u>2250 years ago</u>, the Romans had conquered most of Italy and were starting to build an empire by invading <u>other lands</u>. By about <u>2100 years ago</u> the Romans had taken over much of Gaul — an area where countries like France, Belgium and the Netherlands are today.

About <u>2060 years ago</u>, a powerful Roman leader called <u>Julius Caesar</u> tried to conquer Gaul completely. Some of the Celts in <u>Britain</u> supported the people in Gaul — they didn't want to see them conquered by the Romans.

Look at where <u>Britain</u> and <u>Gaul</u> are on this map.

Why might it have been difficult for the Romans to keep control of Gaul if they didn't have control of Britain?

What do you think Julius Caesar did to solve this problem?

'Gallia' was the Roman name for Gaul.

Britain

Gaul

Rome

Gold and glory

Julius Caesar decided he would try to invade and conquer <u>Britain</u> too. One of the reasons for this was he was worried that the British tribes might help the Gauls to <u>fight against</u> the Romans. This wasn't the only reason though. The Romans thought that Britain had lots of <u>gold</u>, <u>silver</u>, <u>lead</u>, <u>copper</u> and <u>tin</u>. These were metals that the Romans wanted. They also liked the <u>glory</u> of conquering new lands.

History begins

Up until now, everything in this book has been about prehistory — the time <u>before</u> people <u>wrote</u> things down. The Romans could read and write, so when they came to Britain <u>prehistory ended</u> and <u>history began</u>. The Romans also used <u>dates</u> to say when things happened. The dates we use today are based on a system invented during the time of the Romans.

Time ticks on...

We use BC and AD dating to say when things happened.

<u>BC</u> means 'Before Christ'. It's the time <u>before the birth of Christ</u>.

<u>AD</u> means 'Anno Domini'. It's all the time <u>after BC</u>.

The birth of Christ was over 2000 years ago, so all the years for over 2000 years have been AD. So the year 2014 is really AD 2014.

> The man who invented this system was a <u>Christian</u> — that's why it's based on the year that Jesus Christ was thought to be born.

Let's have a look at a timeline showing 'BC' and 'AD' dating...

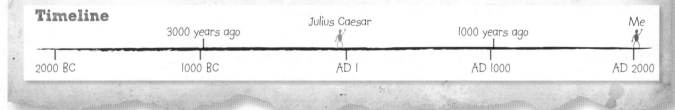

Timeline

| 2000 BC | 3000 years ago 1000 BC | Julius Caesar AD 1 | 1000 years ago AD 1000 | Me AD 2000 |

The end of prehistory – a new era begins

This book gives you an idea of life in <u>prehistoric Britain</u>. It's <u>hard</u> to find out what it was like — there are no written records and most of the evidence has rotted away. The arrival of the Romans was the start of a new period, but that's a tale for another time...

Glossary

AD	Stands for 'Anno Domini'. It's the time after the birth of Christ. For example, Queen Elizabeth II was born 1926 years after Christ, so she was born in AD 1926.
alliance	Where groups agree to work together to help each other.
archaeologist	A person who studies history and prehistory.
awl	A tool used to make holes or marks in leather or wood.
BC	Stands for 'Before Christ'. It's the time before the birth of Christ. For example, Julius Caesar was born 100 years before Christ, so he was born in 100 BC.
bronze	A metal made of copper and tin.
Bronze Age	The period of time in Britain which started around 4000 years ago and ended around 2700 years ago. It came after the Copper Age and before the Iron Age.
Celts	The name that's been given to the tribes who lived in Britain during the Iron Age. Celtic tribes also lived in mainland Europe.
cemetery	A place where the remains of people who have died are buried.
climate	What the weather is like in general over a long period of time.
Copper Age	The period of time in Britain which started around 4500 years ago and ended around 4000 years ago. It came after the Neolithic and before the Bronze Age.
copper ore	A type of rock that contains copper.
cremated	When the remains of a person who has died are burnt.
crop	A plant that is grown by farmers on purpose. For example, farmers grow crops of wheat, barley and vegetables.
domesticated	When an animal has been bred to behave in a way that benefits humans. For example, horses have been domesticated so that humans can ride them.
empire	A group of countries that are controlled by one ruler. For example the Roman Empire, the British Empire.

evidence	Things that give us <u>information</u> about something. A piece of evidence could show us <u>what</u> happened, <u>when</u> something happened or <u>why</u> something happened. For example, an <u>iron tool</u> that's <u>2000 years old</u> is <u>evidence</u> that people <u>made tools from iron 2000 years ago</u>.
fertile land	Land which is <u>good</u> for <u>growing crops</u> on.
flint	A <u>hard</u>, <u>shiny rock</u>. When it's <u>hit</u> with something hard it <u>splits</u> into <u>sharp flakes</u>, so it can be used to make simple <u>tools</u> and <u>weapons</u>.
forage	To <u>search</u> for <u>food</u> to eat.
fossil	The <u>remains</u> or the <u>shape</u> of an <u>animal</u>, <u>plant</u> or <u>insect</u> left behind in a <u>rock</u>.
Gaul	An area where countries like <u>France</u>, <u>Belgium</u> and parts of the <u>Netherlands</u> are today. The <u>Gauls</u> were a <u>Celtic tribe</u> from Gaul.
glacial period	A <u>period of time</u> when the <u>climate</u> is very <u>cold</u> and the land is covered in <u>glaciers</u>.
glacier	A huge amount of <u>ice</u> that is made from <u>layers</u> and <u>layers</u> of <u>snow</u> building up over years and being <u>squashed</u> together. Glaciers <u>move slowly</u> across the land.
harvest	Where farmers <u>gather the crops</u> they've grown.
hillfort	An area or settlement built on <u>high ground</u> and enclosed within a <u>wall</u>.
historian	A person who studies <u>history</u> and <u>prehistory</u>.
Homo heidelbergensis	A type of <u>early human</u> that lived in Europe, Asia and Africa over <u>half a million</u> years ago.
hunter-gatherer	A person who <u>hunts animals</u> and <u>forages</u> for food. They don't farm.
interglacial period	A <u>period of time between glacial periods</u> when the <u>ice melts</u> and the weather becomes <u>warmer</u>.
Iron Age	The <u>period of time</u> in Britain which <u>started</u> around <u>2700 years ago</u> and <u>ended</u> around <u>2000 years ago</u>. It came after the Bronze Age.
loom	A structure used to <u>weave material</u> on.
mammoth	A <u>large</u>, <u>hairy</u>, <u>elephant-like</u> animal with <u>long</u>, <u>curved tusks</u>.

Mesolithic	The <u>period of time</u> in Britain which <u>started</u> around <u>11 500 years ago</u>, at the <u>end</u> of the <u>last glacial period</u>. It <u>ended</u> around <u>6500 years ago</u> when people started <u>farming</u>. The Mesolithic was part of the <u>Stone Age</u>.
Neolithic	The <u>period of time</u> in Britain which <u>started</u> around <u>6500 years ago</u>, when people <u>started farming</u>. It <u>ended</u> around <u>4500 years ago</u>, when people started using <u>metals</u> for tools and weapons. The Neolithic was part of the <u>Stone Age</u>.
prehistory	The time before people started <u>writing</u>. In Britain, prehistory <u>ended</u> when the Romans arrived, about <u>2000 years ago</u>.
primary source	A source that is <u>from the period of time</u> being studied. For example, <u>bones</u> or <u>tools</u>.
ritual	An act or a number of acts performed as part of a <u>ceremony</u>.
Romans	People from <u>Rome</u> or the <u>Roman Empire</u>, who first <u>invaded Britain</u> in 55 BC.
secondary source	A source that <u>isn't</u> from the time being studied. For example, <u>textbooks</u> or <u>websites</u>.
settlement	A <u>place</u> where people <u>live</u>. Settlements can be <u>small</u> (e.g. just a few huts), or <u>very large</u>. Some settlements are <u>permanent</u> (people live in them all the time) and some are <u>temporary</u> (people live in them some of the time).
sickle	A hand-held <u>tool</u> used to <u>harvest crops</u>.
source	A piece of <u>evidence</u>.
Stone Age	The <u>period of time</u> in Britain when people used <u>stone tools</u>. It <u>ended</u> around <u>4500 years ago</u> when people started using <u>metals</u> for tools and weapons. The <u>Mesolithic</u> and the <u>Neolithic</u> were part of the Stone Age.
summer solstice	The <u>longest day</u> of the year. In Britain it's near the <u>end of June</u>.
timeline	A line showing the <u>dates</u> that <u>important events</u> happened. The dates are shown in the order that they happened.
tsunami	A <u>huge wave</u> caused by a <u>big disturbance</u> to water. For example, an earthquake underneath the sea could cause a tsunami.
winter solstice	The <u>shortest day</u> of the year. In Britain it's near the <u>end of December</u>.